SPEAKING
WITH
MAGPIES

SPEAKING WITH MAGPIES

Poems

James McGrath

SUNSTONE PRESS

SANTA FE

Cover: "Speaking with Magpies," 2002, in the collection of Mary Randlett, Olympia, Washington, acrylic and ink on canvas.
All brush and ink drawings by James McGrath.

Magpie petroglyph image from Indian Petroglyph State Park, Three Rivers, New Mexico.

Thanks to Frances Hunter, Santa Fe, New Mexico poet friend, who edited and assisted in the preparation of Speaking With Magpies.

© 2007 by James McGrath. All rights reserved.

No part of this book may be reproduced in any form or by any electronic or mechanical means including information storage and retrieval systems without permission in writing from the publisher, except by a reviewer who may quote brief passages in a review.

Sunstone books may be purchased for educational, business, or sales promotional use. For information please write: Special Markets Department, Sunstone Press, P.O. Box 2321, Santa Fe, New Mexico 87504-2321.

Library of Congress Cataloging-in-Publication Data

McGrath, James, 1928-
  Speaking with magpies : poems / by James McGrath.
    p. cm.
  ISBN 978-0-86534-581-2 (pbk. : alk. paper)
  I. Title.

PS3613.C497S64 2007
811'.6--dc22
                                    2007008449

WWW.SUNSTONEPRESS.COM
SUNSTONE PRESS / POST OFFICE BOX 2321 / SANTA FE, NM 87504-2321 /USA
(505) 988-4418 / ORDERS ONLY (800) 243-5644 / FAX (505) 988-1025

 **DEDICATION**

To those who hear their voices
in the orchards of the world,
who find their image
in puddles after rain,
who fly with clouds,
one day a raving magpie,
another day a dove.

To those poet friends
who are willing to speak
their pain and their joys
with words that reveal
life as it is.

To the memory of those
who have loved me,
who have left me
standing in the shadows
listening to the heartbeats of magpies.

 **CONTENTS**

Introduction / 9

MORNING TALK

15 / A Poet Searching Under Clouds
16 / There is a Magpie Inside Me
18 / In the Shadow of the Mountains
19 / Four Blossoms
21 / When Rivers Run Over Their Banks
22 / Crusts of Bread
23 / A Quiet Poem
24 / Awakening on a September Morn
26 / A Week in the Round Tin Tub
28 / Cutting Through the Bark
29 / One Sweet Apple
30 / This is the Day
31 / Echoes of Shadows
32 / In a Book of Poems
33 / Love Poems
34 / Winter in La Cieneguilla
35/ /The Heart's Sheepdog
36 / The Poet: Three Poems
39 / The Truth of Mountains
40 / Family Portraits

HIGH NOON SONGS

43 / Gifts of the Magpie
44 / Across Dry Grasses
46 / The Shape of a Heart
47 / Hand in Hand
48 / The Snake and I
49 / The Gift of a Poem
50 / Rattlesnakes
51 / The Only Darkness Here
52 / Mango Juice and Pigeons for a Stranger
54 / What Neruda Didn't Write
55 / In the Time of Drought
56 / At the Bridge to Juarez
58 / Beyond Columbus
59 / Tenderness
60 / We Speak in the Silence of Summer
62 / Inviting Sunflowers
63 / Close Enough to Touch

AFTERNOON POEMS

67 / Speaking With Magpies
69 / You'll Turn to Lichen
70 / We Were Two Crossword Puzzles
72 / Raspberries to Keep the Heart Beating
73 / The Ouroboros
74 / Picnic
76 / Flying With Icarus
78 / It Carries Us Lightly
80 / At the End of Summer
81 / Searching for Icarus
82 / The Grand Tour
84 / Learning to Play the Lyre with Orpheus
86 / O'Keeffe's Assistant
88 / Evacuee
89 / Waiting for the Call
90 / Ripening in the Orchard
91 / Putting the Fire to Rest

NIGHT VOICES

95 / A Poem from the Magpie
96 / A Gift of Stars
97 / The Archeologist as Full Moon
99 / At Monk's Pub
100 / A Poet Returning Home
101 / The Hand on My Shoulder
102 / The Flower that Steals the Sun
103 / The Fifth of July, 2005
104 / Where are the Words
105 / Blue of Baghdad
106 / Listening for Their Voices
108 / Brothers
109 / On a Carpet of Woven Flowers
110 / To Celebrate the Dark
112 / The Longest Winter
113 / Returning to the Orchard
114 / One Last Poem
115 / When My Shadow Sleeps
116 / I Don't Need Two Lives
117 / Learning About Fire
118 / In the Sounds of Light
119 / He Died Before I Could Hold Him
121 / In Remembrance
122 / The Last Word of My Pen

INTRODUCTION

In 1946, in Ellensburg, I met my first magpie. I was a beginning college student in the high desert country of Central Washington State, home to coyotes and magpies. My first floor dormitory room overlooked an irrigation ditch. My desk was just under the window. The irrigation ditch was a world of bird activity, especially with the magpies who seemed to be the caretakers of the area. They would pick up candy wrappers, apple cores, bits of shredded term papers, string.

By early Spring, I was well acquainted with magpie activities. In particular, I looked for the one with the exceedingly long tail feathers, a decidedly cheerleader strut and blinding iridescence. We had eyed each other through the window on his morning patrols. Before long, he had jumped onto the windowsill and pecked the window, eyeing my blue fountain pen and the shine from my wristwatch.

When the weather became warm enough, I could open my window on windless days. One Saturday in late March, most of the Cle Elum, Yakima and Union Gap students had gone home for the weekend and my window was open. That tapping magpie jumped up onto the sill. Eyed me. Turned his head this way, that way. Made a rasping sound then a soft clacking-cluck. I nodded. Tried to imitate him. He rasped. Clacked-clucked. Nodded. Stepped across the windowsill onto the open dictionary. Rasped. We shared peanut butter cookies and shelled sunflower seeds. I was not very good at rasping but managed some acceptable clacking clucks. I gave him my red comb when he left.

He returned the next day. It was Sunday. He tapped on the window. I opened it, he hopped in. We clacked and clucked, finished the cookies and seeds. He left with the yellow Ludwig Drugstore pencil.

These visitations became weekend events. I did not tell my roommate why I wanted to stay on the campus every weekend when he invited me to his home in Union Gap.

By the time the term ended in June, I was becoming quite proficient in Magpie. I decided to stay for Summer School.

Magpie and I would strut along the irrigation ditch in the mornings before other students were up. One humdrum, dispirited day, he was walking ahead. Stopped. Looked back, clacked, flew a short distance. Stopped. Looked back to be certain I was following. He took me to the edge of a willow thicket. Made new calling sounds. Flicked his tail into a prismatic blue-black fan. Out of the willows came six, seven, eight rasping magpies. They preened and clacked, all iridescent in the sun. I sat down, excited, stunned. Some jumped on my legs, my shoulders, beaked through my hair, rasping, telling me, "Welcome. We have stories and poems to share with you."

That was sixty years ago. I am in New Mexico now. On quiet days, I go into my orchard below my adobe house in La Cieneguilla where the magpies have gathered their lives together into their nests. We speak of important things. It doesn't look like this conversation will be ending soon.

Speaking With Magpies is my second book of poetry with Sunstone Press. It is my gathering of lost keys, string, droppings, bits of insulation written in my New Mexico nest when I am not in Ireland, Greece or back at the irrigation ditch.

—James McGrath
La Cieneguilla, Santa Fe, New Mexico

Morning Talk
There is a Magpie Inside Me

A Poet Searching Under Clouds

I went to the mountain to welcome Spring.

The day was lying softly under clouds,
    heavy, silent, next to stones.

I waited until the rising of the sun,
    when the flames of flowers erupted.

21 April 2005

There is a Magpie Inside Me
—for my daughter Jeni Keleen Viney

There is a magpie inside me
      next to the turtle and the dragonfly.

It speaks at odd hours.
      At night it awakens my dreaming foxes.

It flies to far-off places,
      holding clouds tight
      among its feathers,
      its beak carrying juniper berries.

It builds its nest in Spring
      before all snow melts.
      It listens to the seeping sounds
      of Winter weeping.

There is a magpie inside me
      next to the horse
      and the pterodactyl.

It waits, expecting hummingbirds
      to share their honey.

It preens its wings,
      making shining mirrors
      for iridescent beetles
      and star-eyed gnats.

It never sleeps.

It carries the sun from one horizon
      to the other.

It presses its head to my chest, it sings
of loneliness and wild iris.

12 September 2005
Galisteo, New Mexico

In the Shadow of the Mountains
—for Aida Davis

I invite you to this quiet place.

The shadow of the Sangre de Cristo
        Mountains sprawls across our path.

The morning begins with whispering jays
        and the waving of magpie flags.

We will dance with tumbleweeds
        in the pungency of sage.

At night there are a thousand bright
        windows in the sky
        that the shadow of the mountain
        cannot darken.

16 December 2003

Four Blossoms

ONE

Let me whisper my song in your ear.

It is full of light
        falling through pear blossoms.

It has no words,
        only the warmth of my breathing bees.

TWO

A shadow flies across my feet.

It sings to dandelions.

Doves play their flutes.

Blue grape-hyacinths cluster
        their bright stones.

Somewhere a heart breaks.

THREE

Is it possible
        to sit here longer,
        the buzzing scent of pear and plum
        ringing my body with first light?

Is it possible
        to wait long enough for fruit to ripen,
        when the birds flit from tree to tree,
        searching for home?

Somewhere a heart breaks.

Is it in the West Bank or Basra or Balakot,
      where the remnants of city walls
        are wailing?

           FOUR

What hums in the orchard?

Is it the pear tree chanting?

16 April 2004
Galisteo, New Mexico

When Rivers Ran Over Their Banks
—for my friend Mary Randlett

I celebrate the water-years I lived beside rivers
    rushing through my childhood,
    the years listening to gargling rains
    galumphing down drainpipes.

I smell the years of dampness
    in cedar woodpiles
    woven into woolen Cowichen sweaters
    and the acid of wet chicken feathers.

I hear driftwood carving riverbanks,
    the weeping of moss-covered fences
    and the belch of mulching decay
    in the valley swamps.

In my poems today, I find the writing
    left for me yesterday in sandbars
    by wading birds and crawdads.

I honor the translucent memories,
    born with Northwest floods, inconsolable,
    when rivers ran groping
    over their banks:

    the Skookumchuck
    the Snohomish
    the Queets
    the Puyallup.

                January 2004

Crusts of Bread

My parents stayed on the sidelines,
    watched me grow.
    Rarely said no.
    Rarely said yes.

Mother filling the washing machine,
    hanging sheets, ironing sheets,
    filling lunch pails.

Dad leaving early for work,
    changing oil in the truck,
    returning home in plaster-covered overalls,
    talking to the dog.

My chickens watching for crusts
    in the backyard.

My bread-crusts were a bucket of steamed clams,
    new shoes before school started,
    two weeks without a haircut,
    watching water-skippers on the swamp waters,
    wild blackberry pie.

My chickens were black and white
    like the drawings in my book, *The Deerslayer,*
    or the Saturday matinee, *Lost Horizon.*

        3 October 2005

A Quiet Poem

With a fire burning behind my back,
    small crackles of wet wood,
    a warmth is deepening.

This poem, glowing like a spark,
    ignites words,
    falls from a place
    where I have never been.

This poem fills the room,
    pushes the walls away,
    captures quivering shadows on the floor,
    filters the light in family portraits,
    pulls the sky inside the room,
    fills my eyes with the sound of wind.

I see yellow in the trees by the river.
    The bark of the tree outside the window
    is opening wider, as if to sing.

I fear the tree is a deaf-mute,
    a mask, like this poem.

This is a quiet poem. It speaks without a voice.

I shall let the fire burning behind me
    turn into embers
    before I take the mask away.

                      1 October 2005

Awakening on a September Morn
—*in memory of Aunt Margaret and Uncle Art*

In my uncle and aunt's bedroom
        was a painting
        that I visited on weekends.

Soft colors, a misty blue-eyed lake,
        a lady in gauzy pink,
        her toe almost touching water,
        hazy Greek ruins,
        intriguing to a twelve-year-old.

Aunt Margaret called it September Morn,
        said it was by her favorite French painter,
        Paul Chabas.

I learned later
        it was in the Art Deco style:
        voluptuous colors,
        muted sexuality,
        a hint of heavy breathing.

Aunt Margaret was an artist,
        taught me watercolors,
        took me to the Seattle Art Museum.

The Autumn was our favorite painting time.

On September 2nd, my thirteenth birthday,
        we went to Volunteer Park to paint.
        I looked out of the corner of my eye,
        through the falling chestnut leaves,
        over the flock of feeding pigeons
        and reflecting pool,

hoping to catch the September Morn lady
stepping out of the rhododendrons
and sword ferns,
her finger upright,
motioning me to join her.

3 October 2005

A Week in the Round Tin Tub
—in memory of Uncle Nap and Aunt Sinnie

I was the last to bathe in the round tin tub
    on Saturdays. Aunt Sinnie added a bucket
    of hot water to what was already there,
    bringing the water up to above my belly-button.

On Sundays, when company came, two or three
    chickens were scalded in the round tin tub,
    leaving feathers stuck to the sides
    and sweet, thick chicken smells.

On Mondays, overalls, aprons, long-johns,
    two bottom bed-sheets were washed in it,
    rinsed in the river and hung up
    on the cherry tree branches to dry.

Tuesday night found the tin tub
    on the wood stove, boiling and sealing
    jars of peaches, green beans
    or piccalilli.

Wednesday might be the scrub-the-floor day
    when Uncle Nap and I had to stay out of doors.
    We usually went huckleberry picking
    or agate hunting on the Nuwaukum.

Thursday meant the tin tub was used
    to carry chopped wood. It had two handles
    so it was easy to carry to the woodshed
    next to the kitchen porch.

On Fridays, the tub could be used for most
    anything. I might sit in it for a haircut.
    Aunt Sinnie might shuck corn in it.

Uncle Nap might mix up the pee
from the pee-pots with water for the garden
or make an extra big batch of slop
and mash for the weekend to feed the pigs.

Whatever happened in that tin tub on Fridays,
    I had to bathe in it the next day, hoping
    the cake of Ivory soap was big enough
    to float and not get lost somewhere
    on the bottom.

10 March 2004

Cutting Through the Bark
—for those girls in Edison Grade School

My first pocket-knife
      gave me permission
      to begin carving initials
      into fence posts and trees.

Cherry trees were easy:
      their red bark peeled smoothly
      like a ripe peach.

The trunks of apple and pear trees
      were too heavily ribbed and tough.
      Alder barks were the best.

Never attempt to carve a telephone pole.
      The creosote impregnated outer shell
      is tenacious. It splinters, dulls a knife.

Two initials are easy,
      but in the sixth grade I met Janet Sommers.

It would take twice as long
      to carve JM and JS.
      I intertwined the two J's into a heart:
      very artistic.

Sixty-five years have passed.
      The intertwined heart
      may be covered with moss.
      JS went her way.
      JM remains, cutting through the bark
      with a dull knife of memory.

1 October 2005

One Sweet Apple
—for long-time university friend Clif Ouellette

My memory never stops
    placing its hands on my shoulders,
    whispering,
    I am here.

My memory never stops
    placing one foot before the other,
    stepping on dried leaves,
    crushing dung beetles.

There are shards best left in corners
    to gather dust for darker days
    when the light flickers,
    when footsteps grow weak.

In notebooks that begin with blank pages
    dreams wait for morning or thunder
    to rub their faces clean.

If I read the map in my palm correctly
    I have some years left.

When the snow melts
    and Spring floods come down my road,
    I will wade barefoot in the mud
    so I can feel the sharp teeth
    of broken obsidian spears.

I will call out to the magpies in my orchard:
    I am here.
    Please save one sweet apple for me.
    I promise I won't give it to a stranger.

        13 November 2004

This is the Day
   —for Bill Allan, Jaimi and Grady

This is the day I won't put my pen down.

I want my paper to bleed,
        sing my songs.

I want my fire to ignite the clouds.
        There will be no ashes.
        I'll send the sun home early.

This is the day to rearrange the stars,
        bleed the harvest of kisses
        that leave tattoos on my ear lobes.

This is the day for weaving magic carpets,
        apple juice, broken shoe strings
        and love letters.

No one need know where magpies go
        in snow storms or why rose hips
        keep their eyes open.

There is no waiting for unanswered telephone calls.
        All the lines are busy.

13 January 2005

Echoes of Shadows
—in memory of my friend Marjorie Weiss

Marjorie asked me to write a poem
      titled, Echoes of Shadows.

We had been speaking of our long friendship,
      of painting together near the river,
      of sharing grasses, feathers and sunsets.
      There was the music of seedpods.

We needed to capture a taste of past laughter,
      of moments with a cup of tea,
      of loss in the clouds.
      There were children to hum to.

An echo is the small voice
      hidden under stones that years
      leave behind, moments that add up
      to gardens and walls.
      There were tears to walk with.

And those shadows:
      those shapes of things passing,
      those haunts,
      those voices we heard alone,
      those stops along the way.
      There were journeys to re-map.

I wanted her to know
      she kept the door open
      when the shadows pinned the feet down,
      when their echoes faded.

21 August 2005

In a Book of Poems

I gather stones, rattle papers,
      snap fingers, net fish,
      and when it is over,
      I will press my heart in a book of poems.

Where do words come from:
      tea from woven tea bags,
      fresh, squeezed hot,
      not needing milk or sugar?

The cup is waiting, edged in whispers.
      No one can scrape the pattern away.

She sits, fingering her string of pearls,
      head nodding,
      her eyes Winter persimmons,
      lips torn rose petals.

There must be parsley and peonies
      in bloom.
      I will ask her one more time
      when she awakens.

Today I will spell ageing with an e
      and capitalize Flower Bud.
      A heart will be fading
      in a book of poems.

                    23 November 2004

Love Poems
—for John and Gale Haugse

There was a time
      we would flirt between book covers,
      when a love poem said it all:
      the words, the breathing,
      the glances that burned holes in the night.

Touching stole the silence,
      gave a blush to our conversations,
      left a phantom on the privacy of a living room sofa.

Love letters sealed our lips,
      filled our pockets with visions of dancing dolls.
      When we closed our envelopes,
      our tongues were blue from the words.

Then we walked home together,
      you the sparrow,
      me the magpie.
      We gathered our feathers to make wings
      to fan the coals into flames.

But the clouds gathered,
      wind and rain blew the blossoms off the trees.
      Even the bees starved for lack of nectar.

Now we return to the books,
      read Neruda,
      listen to Mary Oliver,
      wishing we had used stronger glue on our wings.

Tomorrow I will make a cup of tea,
      read my leaves,
      search for a way
      to tie the moon to the mountain top.

9 October 2005

Winter in La Cieneguilla
   —for my friend Marcia Starck

When I go to my car these Winter mornings,
    I find frozen prints left by night animals:
    raccoons, skunks, a coyote.
    Their shadows have disappeared
    with the morning light.

Their tracks are vulnerable as dew.
    The sun will melt them into mud by noon.

When I stop long enough to breathe small clouds,
    I follow those prints across the ripples
    of my garden, beyond the road,
    toward the mountains in the East.

A voice sings to me:
    Look East. Climb the mountains.
    Join the animals.
    Leave your shadows behind.

                        16 January 2005

The Heart's Sheepdog
—for Jerome Bernstein, my Borderland friend

It is in the fierce center of aloneness
      where I can have a conversation with you.

That center holds the choice of risk.
      It is the attentive nucleus,
      the astonishing atom
      of being able to speak.

Here is the place where the heart's sheepdog
      keeps love and loss in formation.

This is not the edge.

It is the center of things.

It is what makes the hawk fly.

It is where the fire holds firm
      in dying embers.

                    16 October 2005

The Poet: Three Poems
 —*for my County Kildare poet friend Liam Aungier*

                ONE

He brought a branch of wild roses
      into the house,
        put them into a pitcher of water,
        waited days for them to bloom.

He should have known
      they would swell up,
      puff out,
      but without birdsong,
      they would never raise their heads,
      never offer their honey-laden breath
      to the carpets,
      to the walls.

They would never burst into bloom.

He should have known
      it was the moon
      that pulled them open,
      and the morning birds
      that sang their yellow petals
      into the shape of a rose.

                TWO

Again and again
      he was lost in the grass.

His legs would grow shorter,
      his feet melt away.

He followed unmarked paths
    between clumps of buttercup
    and grama grass.

He was lost.

He would suck on long stems of mint
    until he turned green.
    His arms waved in time with a nearby dandelion.
    His head became clover,
    buzzing with bees.

He listened for sparrow chatter
    but heard only weeping crickets
    and the rumble of rolling sow bugs.

At last he knew where he belonged.

THREE

He was a poet.

He was alone.
    He wandered,
    stumbled into the blossoms in his orchard,
    searching for pen and paper.

There were butterflies scribbling in the blooms.

His eyes ran along the branches.

He became blind from the fiery white flames.

He held his breath.

His fingers tingled.

The only thing to write on
    was the woven bark of trees.

All he had left was his blood
    and a world of twigs.

And that was enough.

19 May 2005

The Truth of Mountains
—for my poet friend Mary McGinnis

Hold out your hand.

I give you my word.

I squeeze this paper dry of ink,
        vowels crossing the lines in your palm,
        telling your fortune
        that a heart-break can be colored
        in the gentle shades of blue
        that rain brings on hot Summer days.

I will hold out my hand
        to receive your word
        that spells flesh-and-blood
        for as long as I live.

I will take your words to be the truth of mountains.

Once again,
        hold out your hand,
        take my word, breathe on it kindly.
        It may be the fuel
        that gives fire for illuminating
        the space between us.

                      22 November 2005

Family Portraits

There are no curtains at my windows.
    I want faces to appear at daybreak.

In the morning there are no fly-specks to count.
    I've collected the carapaces of beetles
    in a small matchbox.

What surprises there are at high noon,
    gathering into threatening silver spider webs.

Afternoon light rests on the windowsills,
    holding its breath.
    The sun has stolen its reflection
    once again.

When lamplight breaks the window glass at night
    childhood fears may enter
    to frighten the family portraits.

23 November 2005

High Noon Songs
Close Enough to Touch

Gifts of the Magpie

There is a raspberry in the eye
      of every magpie.

It lies ripening under black glass feathers
      of crows who scratch and prowl
      between the night and frightened pears.

There is a peacock in the iridescent flight
      of every magpie.
      The colors will blind me
      if I hold them too close.

There is a razor scent of marigold
      in the flight of every magpie.

It cuts through the fog bank
      of County Clare;
      it piles stones on hillsides
      where prayers are left behind.

There is the taste of lime on the breath
      of every magpie.

.
There is a poem in the silence
      of every magpie.
      It fills the space in the trees,
      left by fallen apples.

20 August 2005

Across Dry Grasses
—*for my friend Sheila Gershen*

At high noon
        the stones hold the day's heat
        that I will touch only with my eyes.

I will keep the soft-feathered songs
        of a hidden bird, vibrating
        in my poem.

This hot July day has a new scent
        I will roll into a ball
        of beeswax to melt slowly
        on a cold Winter's night
        when you are sleeping.

I will keep that scent
        for a pair of magpies
        scolding in the orchard.
        It is the scent on your shoulders
        of ripening apples.

Movements in this moment
        crawl from my pen
        to tell you that my eyes
        are locust leaves, my feet
        are the stones in the path
        to my door; my fingers
        are for dipping into bowls of water
        to sprinkle you with the sweet water
        that hummingbirds love.

I do not hear the galloping of horses
    across dry grasses.

Have you seen the breathing white light
    of the spider web in the wild rosebush?

Let us weave it together
    before the sun blinds us.

10 July 2005

The Shape of a Heart
—for Coral Venske Luzzi
and Pat Playford Torkleson

There are no voices in the past twenty-four hours,
        only echoes
        made of indiscernible sounds,
        like voices heard through old shoes
        that have hiked unnamed mountains
        and vanished jungles.

I want to wear the next twenty-four hours
        as a long soft overcoat
        of woven sea foam or traveling clouds,
        each pocket stuffed with plain white paper,
        waiting to be burned to ashes
        by heated words and broken promises.

I want to inscribe the next twenty-four hours
        into the shape of a heart
        on the sidewalk outside Edison Grade School
        where I learned to spell tomorrow
        with two r's
        so that when I walk there again
        to play hop-scotch
        my feet won't stumble.

26 November 2003

Hand in Hand
—for my daughter Jain Kellain Middaugh

This is the hand that caressed
      the glowing heads of two daughters
      that now brushes the purring of two cats.

Between two daughters and two cats
      have been years of holding the hands of others,
      years of exclaiming in paint and words.

I read the lines in this hand
      to see if my lifeline ends in the same place,
      there where the wrist begins.

This hand has lost a bit of its strength
      for twisting nuts and bolts,
      for tying thick sisal ropes to trees.
      It keeps the skill for ribbons and strings.

Today memory holds both hands lightly,
      the two hands that tied ribbons
      in the hair of two daughters
      when the three of us played together,
      this hand and this hand
      full of two daughters.

16 January 2005

The Snake and I

I've done cruel things
       like stealing, lying, lusting
        and showing anger at being loved.

I climbed over the fence around the Garden,
       took bites of apple after apple.
       I threatened the unblinking snake
       with beheading
       if it did not shed its skin.

I wanted to begin my day, a bud
       not waiting for the sunrise.

I wanted to run fresh and fire-new
       across the world, leaving no ashes.

I wanted to hold the breath
       of my children in my arms
       during their Winter days.

But I tired easily.

I never gave a name to the snake,
       the one I met in nightmares
       that leered behind me
       in freshly-washed mirrors.

But we have become friends,
       the snake and I.

                      22 June 2004

The Gift of a Poem
—for my poet friend Catherine Ferguson

In this April garden where tulips bloom
        as yellow and red cups of Spring wine,
        where columbines hold back colors
        on frosty mornings,
        where cat-mint clumps together
        in gray-green fur,
        I plant you.

I want you to be here
        when I enter the morning light
        with a pitcher of water
        for the newly-arrived orioles.

I want to plant you here
        next to a budding pear tree
        with an early iris kiss.

I want to flower my day
        full of your forsythia brightness,
        your body-armor of honeysuckle.

I want you to apple-blossom me,
        to fill my pockets
        with the sprouting seeds
        of the morning's oregano and parsley.

I will plant you in this garden.

You will erupt with the lark,
        hovering,
        laying your flower-filled days here
        for me to feather a poem
        as my gift for you.

23 April 2005
Galisteo, New Mexico

Rattlesnakes

They come every Summer.

Their brown and silver diamonds blaze
        among tomatoes, marigolds
        and blooming cholla.

I watch them flow among silent gray
        basalt stones, their rattling songs
        a hint of rain.

I see them curl into undulating spirals,
        their heads sliced open
        by a swift black tongue.

Their amber-coated eyes never close.
        They shoot a primitive fear
        into the air.

If I pause nearby long enough,
        they know I love them.
        They glide away to a peaceful place.

I walk on with a rapid heartbeat,
        hinting of rain.

22 June 2004

The Only Darkness Here
—for my poet friend Morgan Farley

Across the field of buttercups,
    globes of pink clover,
    clumps of stinging nettle,
    a cuckoo haunts the hawthorn hedge.

Constellations of white daisies huddle
    among frescoes of lichened limestone boulders.

A single dandelion is the lonely eye
    of this place,
    the cuckoo its melancholy voice.

The only darkness here
    is the flock of black crows:
    they sit in pairs
    on the parapet of Corcomroe Abbey
    watching for ghosts in the hungry fields.

29 May 2005
Corcomroe Abbey
County Clare, Ireland

Mango Juice and Pigeons for a Stranger
—for my poet friend Enid Howarth

I've seen you among papaya and eucalyptus trees.

Fog blooms at your feet,
        red poppies in your cheeks.

Are you dreaming of bird feathers
        or do you wish to ride seahorses?

If you hold my hand,
        I would share eight endless days with you.

The first day would be for picking mangoes.
        We would be sweeter with mango juice
        on our lips.

The second and third days
        we would race with rabbits,
        make songs of the wailing of coyotes.
        We would put hummingbirds behind our ears.

On the fourth day we will wait
        until the moon is resting
        in the poinsettia bed.
        We will blush together,
        you, me and the poinsettia.

Day five is the day for laughter.
        Let us bare our feet,
        put ribbons on our ankles,
        sequins on our knees,
        dance among ripe grapes and marigolds,
        crushing oregano and lavender.

Do you like pigeons?
>   On the sixth day we will try to catch pigeons.
>   The pigeons on the corner of Hidalgo and Canal
>   seem to be waiting for us.
>   They are well fed, lethargic.
>   We will coax them with peanuts and poetry.

Day seven is for chasing darkness.
>   Please bring a roman candle and eggshells.
>   We will meet at the statue of Christobal Colon,
>   encourage him to return to his ship:
>   he has been standing there, stiff in his bronze,
>   frightening children, oppressing grandmothers,
>   long enough.

What would you like to do on our eighth day?
>   What have we left undone?

If we look into a dusty mirror together,
>   you with mango juice on your lips,
>   me with a pigeon on my shoulder,
>   we will write in the dust
>   what we don't have time for
>   and never use the word *stranger* again.

>   *4 January 2005*
>   *San Miguel de Allende, Mexico*

What Neruda Didn't Write
—for my poet friend Marjorie Agosin

The carpet of moonlight
      that rolls down my road
      when the snow has silenced footsteps;

      memories that lie in wait
      for the morning dew to wash their hearts;

      being without skin,
      I am about to be stolen by sunlight

      to lie naked among ripe pears,
      bees humming,
      where only the blind world
      will look at me and see nothing.

These are phosphorescent things,
      spots of deer-light on ripe blueberries.

30 September 2005

In the Time of Drought
—for my friend Stewart Udall in memory of Lee

After the lake I drink from dries up,
> I will make the lake bed my home
> until the rains come again.

I will gather obsidian points
> in the ancestral wallows.

Dust-filled bird bones
> for making flutes
> will wail songs of water.

At dusk I will sit in silence,
> waiting for migrating geese
> to hover over the dryness.
> I will have only a single thermos
> of water to share with them.

How long can they stay with me?

I shall play my bird-bone flute for them.
> They will gather around me
> in concentric circles.

They will murmur of lakes filled
> with clouds, sing of lost trails
> and ancient resting places,
> where only cities grow.

They will describe rivers flowing
> with watercress, ponds of duckweed
> and reeds.

And when they leave at dawn,
> I will fly with them.

6 March 2004

At the Bridge to Juarez

Down 285
    through Las Cruces to El Paso,
    then we wait at the bridge to Juarez.

Remembrances of the slaughtered women from the *maquiladoras*
    confront us, lacerate, torture our ears,
    stumble with us across the Rio Grande.

It's like watching a burning house
    through a double-paned window,
    hearing no crackles of flames
    or sizzles of wet wood burning.

Pain is in glances of eyes
    at the *mercado*,
    in reflections on polished
    purple eggplants,
    in dew on ripe orange papayas.

At the bridge to Juarez there is no turning back,
    no putting the mourning in my back pocket
    where my wallet has worn holes.

Migrating butterflies never stop here.
    They fly at 2000 feet.
    No one knows their real number.
    Some say as many as 500 million
    find peace at El Rosario Sanctuary.

When they die
> they fall to the ground
> without a sound,
> > their wings folded together.

> > > > *22 January 2005*

maqiladoras: sweatshop factories
mercado: marketplace

Beyond Columbus

We thought Columbus, New Mexico,
    would be a safe place to cross.

There was no time to share our papaya
    with the gringo Border Patrol.

They searched our *bolsa,*
    the one embroidered and sequined
    with Our Lady of Guadalupe.

They took our fruit and seeds.

They made us pay for our extra pair of shoes
    and the T-shirts;
    they said: **These are imports.**

We couldn't change our remaining pesos
    at the Crossing Office;
    they said: **Go to a bank.**

The children were hungry.

The people at McDonald's yelled: **No food.**
    Come back with dollars.
    Stay away from the garbage cans.

Columbus returned home
    after discovering America.

        22 January 2005

bolsa: shopping bag

Tenderness
    —for my poet friend Lonnie Howard

I will not give my loneliness away too soon.

I will gather the apples my trees drop
    because there is no one to pick them.

I will shine them bright
    by bringing light
        through my fingers into my home.

And when you come for tea,
    we will share an apple
        while the enduring moon touches
        the mountain of our tenderness.

        12 October 2005

We Speak in the Silence of Summer
—for Bob Hudson and Mavis Jukes

A magpie is nesting in my orchard.
      Three vibrating eggs are lodged
      among fingers of string and twigs,
      eyes of bottle caps, bleached bones,
      ears of horse hair, fragments of yellow insulation.

Each day I climb the apple tree,
      where the nest ripens,
      searching for lost dreams,
      boyhood memories, marbles,
      airline-seat tickets, old passports.

I find in the nest things not done,
      kisses unaccepted,
      good-byes unuttered,
      promises kept but lost
      in the mix of rubbish and fragments.

Oh, yes! There are also cookie crumbs,
      Indian beaded belts, a taste
      of halvah, feathered headdresses
      and pages from unread Agosin novels,
      beauty and truth in large warm handfuls
      of light and darkness.

We speak in the silence of Summer, petals
      falling, Autumn fruit ripening
      while the sky hums.

I won't take a single twig
    or button from the nest:
    I don't want that nesting black and white rapscallion
    to spend next Spring looking
    for a single lost treasure, as I have.

The magpies will leave
    their accumulated memories
    in their nests.
    If I don't translate them into poems
    I am afraid memory might forget me.

8 August 2005

Inviting Sunflowers
—for Donna Salazar

Mid-August, the air crumbles
    under the stomping of afternoon thunder.

Crickets and night moths
    hidden under hot stones
    wait their turns to crack open the hardness,
    to brush against window screens,
    to blind the moon.

The warriors of thunder retreat,
    taking their bows and arrows with them.
    They fly over picnic grounds and cornfields,
    inviting sunflowers to raise their faces.

18 August 2004

Close Enough to Touch
—for Julie Reid

The gate is left open for you.

There is no latch to catch
      at the sleeve of your coat.

There is no rust on the hinges
      to frighten birds.

It is a simple gate. You must remember it.

Wooden slats rubbed smooth
      by Winter storms.

Morning glories climbing
      in its ribs.

If you swing it slowly,
      it sings of penstemon and phlox.

I never close our gate.

It is agape, waiting for your loneliness
      when you come again.

2 July 2005
Galisteo, New Mexico

Afternoon Poems
Flying with Icarus

Speaking With Magpies
—for Bill Wiley

Magpies collect the world.

In their nests of woven twigs,
        they hold lost rings,
        old letters, duck feathers,
        cat fur, identification tags
        from neighborhood dogs,
        broken talons of owls,
        Tafoya's lost keys.

They sit on fence posts gathering stories,
        voices of spotted towhees,
        shadows of red-tailed hawks,
        passing clouds,
        whispering hisses of snakes,
        twistings of lizards,
        the agony of polluted lichens.

Their tail feathers,
        longer than their lumpy bodies,
        are usually frayed from leaving messages,
        poems in the road dust and sandbars,
        arguments in the apple trees.

Their stories are carried
        from orchard to orchard,
        across mountains,
        through windows,
        held in the laps of children,
        caught in the coats of bears,
        etched in the spots of lynx.

Magpies are the Mevlana Jelaheddin Rumi
    of the natural world, waiting
    to give their hoards away
    to those who listen to their chattering wisdom,
    who write poems or sit on stones,
    loving the world as it is.

10 November 2004

You'll Turn to Lichen
 —for my poet friend Susan McDevitt

In the ruins that press against the Burren
   of County Clare
   live spirits
   cloaked in lichens:
   white lichens for night,
   yellow lichens for day.

These ruins, open to the sky,
   send long trails of psalms
   through nettles in the graveyards:
   Come visit us. Come sit.

These ruins are welcoming places:
   open doorways,
   open windows with stone sills and lintels
   of carved cinquefoil and hazel leaves.

These are open abodes
   where silence lies in dark corners,
   where the Conleys, the Mahonys,
   the Keanes are voiceless.

Although there are wagtails and marsh orchids nearby,
   strangers do not linger long here.

An old man near St. Brigit's Well said:
   You mustn't stay too long
   in these places.
   You'll turn to lichen:
   white lichen at night,
   yellow lichen in the day.

      2 June 2005
      Ballyvaughan,
      County Clare, Ireland

We Were Two Crossword Puzzles

No need to ask if there was a double life
        between us.

It's what we got used to,
        creating habits to start the day
        after the darkness:
        the nice things we said
        to keep the hours open,
        the careful actions,
        testing the waters for directions.

We didn't want to startle ourselves
        or open cracks to fall into.

We didn't want to nail a secret
        on the wall of the bedroom so it bled.

I think we wanted to leave crumbs
        from the warm bread we broke at first.

We had hoped the crumbs might be
        the yeast for bigger, better loaves
        to share when it began to get dark
        and there were no constellations to read.

We came to one another with our double lives.

        Perhaps we expected them to merge,
        to be put together into a completed
        crossword puzzle that would be our map
        to who we really were.

As time went on, we discovered
    there were two crossword puzzles,
    not just one,
    and we had squares to fill in by ourselves,
    squares that had no clues to the answers.

Today when I open the box
    where I keep my crossword puzzle,
    I find some of the answers
    in those squares have changed.

    Some answers have faded beyond recognition.
    Some are polished and shining.
    Some are eyes that have closed,
    tired from staring too long.

September 2004

Raspberries to Keep the Heart Beating

There was no romance
        in the raspberry fields of Puyallup
        to stain our young hearts.

Those were serious days,
        filling our trays to earn money
        for groceries or a pair of shoes.

Those were growing-up years
        when Summer was living chores.

We made a game of who could fill
        their boxes first, who could go longest
        without eating the first berry.

Summer life was like this:
        filling boxes of our hours
        with family duty
        so when the boxes were full
        I could wander off
        into the neighborhood swamp
        to count flies on skunk cabbage,
        collect feathers of nesting ducks,
        build dreams that would not have words
        until years later.

Now, the Puyallup raspberries
        are hidden in layers of ashes
        that have turned cold,
        but there is enough blood from them
        to keep the heart beating.

8 January 2006

The Ouroboros

He couldn't see beyond his shadow.

He kept his shoulders pressed
      against the aging trees in his garden.

When I looked at him,
      searched in his eyes,
      I never saw his transparencies,
      the colored gels of his days.

I wanted to be in his world.
      He kept me out.

It was as if my father held his own hands.

Oh! He worked hard enough.
      Too hard.
      He wore himself out
      until he could no longer
      shed his skin.

When the time came for him to fight,
      he stored his guns.
      He filled his creel with lead sinkers
      and trout flies,
      left the house mid-afternoon.
      Never referred to local road maps.
      Never asked me to follow him.

It is getting late. The road is shorter.
      I'd like him to answer my question
      before the stars fall.

Why did he walk in circles?

26 February 2005

Picnic
—for Margaret Atwood

After cars whirred past,
      black feathers rippled across the road,
      flew into the picnic basket.

They came alone without sound or map.
      They made a trembling mosaic
      among the sliced cucumbers
      and sweet Walla Walla onions.

There was talk of ants and birdsong,
      adult talk of war and peace.

No one noticed the children
      gathering the black feathers
      that fluttered among salads and fried chicken.

The children mounted black wings
      on each other's shoulders.
      They made the sound of wind
      and flapping wings.

The children climbed into a nearby hemlock tree,
      calling one another by name.
      They reached the top branches
      high above their arguing parents.
      They arranged themselves in flight formation.

One by one they jumped.
      Black feathers rippled from the tree top,
      flew into the picnic basket.

They fell without sound or map.

They made a trembling mosaic
        among the sliced cucumbers,
        sweet Walla Walla onions,
        and babbling adults.

                22 August, 2004

Flying With Icarus

He said we won't hold hands.

He said we'll fly through clouds.

He said think of the wax as candlelight.

He said listen to what the birds whisper
    when they fly close to you.

He said each breath you take in comes through me.

He said keep your eyes on the earth,
    name the mountains.

He said he had never flown before.

He said I was very brave. He wanted to marry me.

He said his garden was full of blue iris, blue as my eyes.

He said when we get home we'll count
    the feathers that remain on our bodies.

He said I'll count yours, you'll count mine.

I remember how his body heated up,
    how his feathers tore off, chasing hawks.

I remember how his arms splayed out, arching,
    then circling into Autumn leaves.

I remember how he wailed at the earth
    as it came to meet him.

I remember how he became smaller and smaller,
his voice a sweet, single note.

How he called my name.

2 May 2004

It Carries Us Lightly
—for Aunt Margaret and Uncle Joe

What landscape blooms under the blue sky
        of my eyes?

Let me paint a picture for you.

I can see through wind-torn trees,
        around corners of roofless stone houses,
        into doorways without doors.
        White lichens are the lace curtains now.

Walk the Irish land with me, stepping
        over sparks of pink heather,
        nettles nibbling our ankles.

We will sit on limestone horses,
        peel bitter-scented bark
        from hazel walking sticks.

When we come to small gray cairns,
        we will find empty snail shells
        and black and white paintings
        in raven droppings.

A lark will be hovering, keeping her distance,
        drawing our eyes up to where she calls
        to rabbits and ghosts of potato farmers.

It is a land that harbors sadness,
        unafraid to cry or to feel lost,
        a land of hungry grasses
        that twist and flutter at my sighing.

It is a land where the names on the gravestones
      of our ancestors hold light,
      where empty roadsides bloom
      with red tears of fuchsia,
      where salty winds fill our ears
      with the sounds of tin pipes
      and the tight strings of fiddles.

When we walk on this land together,
      it carries us lightly,
      as if we belong here
      as if we have been here before.

7 February 2004

At the End of Summer

I want to gather these hot Summer days
      into my storeroom
      like letters for Winter reading.

I want to keep them in the organized way
      that I save seeds
      of cosmos and hollyhocks.

I want to wrap myself in the memory
      of watermelon juice
      and the smell of settling dust,
      pummeled by afternoon rain.

But the sounds of a small animal
      on the roof above my kitchen
      recalls your tapping on the train window
      as the morning fog lifted,
      tapping the code
      that the world had ended.

8 August 2004

Searching for Icarus
    —for my poet friend Frances Hunter

They didn't know where he fell,
    never found his body.
    His father's arms were not strong enough
    to catch him.

They say he fell into the sea,
    that he is there,
    waving in the currents
    with kelp and seahorses.

They say he was rescued by swans
    flying South.

They say he circles the earth each Winter
    as snowflakes.

Oh! I searched. I thought I'd found him
    in soft clay,
    ready to be transformed.

On nights,
    when blossoms begin to fall,
    I hear him weeping in my orchard.

        23 April 2005

The Grand Tour
—for my poet friend Judith Toler

My road has stones and potholes.

It branches off into grass, horsetails,
        mullein and a plot of wild roses,
        where birds nest in the Spring.

Just beyond, to the right,
        is a grove of early-blooming plums,
        edging a broken fence and an orchard,
        where poets read in good weather.

Leroy ropes an orange gate to a post
        to keep two face-nuzzling horses
        in the four-acre field, where they run
        from the gate to the river.

A hazel-wood memory of willows borders
        the river. Unnamed plants thrive
        in the undergrowth. Mysterious trails
        press down any grasses. Strong branches
        snatch at my sleeves when I walk by.

The river's edge eats and gurgles
        at a bare-rooted cottonwood that shares
        its map-meandering with a blue heron.

Footprints of deer mark gravel bars at the bend
        of the river.
        Raccoons have made bowls in sand-pockets
        for resting.

If I begin early in the morning,
> I can reach the river before the moon rises.

After I return home, I will write a poem.

> *12 October 2005*

Learning to Play the Lyre with Orpheus
—for Michael and Evangelia "Lisa" Lucas
and Aphrodite "Titi" Andreopoulou

We met at Delphi.

He was weeping under an olive tree
        dropping its November black tears
        near the sacred spring.

He said sweeten your fingers with Leros honey.

He said hold your lyre as you would hold starlight.

He said touch the strings as you would caress
        the cheek of your first love.

He said choose songs to guard *kikni* flying south.

He said be gentle, believe your music hushes nightingales..

He said welcome death with your lyre.

I remember how the olive and cypress trees
        grew silent, how the clouds stopped moving.

I remember the purring of the cats of Olympus.

I remember the empty nest of *helidonia* erupting into song.

I remember the valley filled with the cloying
        heavy scent of asphodel.

I wanted to creep into the realm of the dead
        at the end of the world,
        scream at Orpheus: **Don't look back.**

I would have covered his eyes with my tattered *mathili*.

I would have played my lyre for the wild nymphs
    so they would not tear him apart.

I would have taken his place.

22 September 2005

kikni: swans
helidonia: swallows
mathili: cloth carried by Greek folk dancers

O'Keeffe's Assistant

Miss O'Keeffe was like a large beetle in the patio,
>dressed in black.

She hovered in the doorway
>or sat on the cold corner *banco*
>and rolled a smooth gray stone
>on her shiny over-ironed lap.

She stirred gesso to the consistency
>of her sourdough biscuit batter.

She closely watched each tack
>I hammered in to fasten the canvas
>to the stretcher, first one side,
>then the opposite side, hoping
>I would get the canvas
>straight and tight.

She didn't speak much to me;
>she'd hand the brush to me,
>motioning: *Brush this way,*
>*not that way.*

Or she'd say incomplete sentences:
>*If you would do this . . .*
>with a wave of a hand, or
>*I'd like you to . . .*
>with a twist of a shoulder.

I set the gessoed panel in the sun far away
>from the *chamisa*. I was afraid
>windblown fluff might stick to its surface.

She drank water from the same blue glass
    every day, the glass with her dried
    black oil-paint fingerprints on it.
    Just before lunch, I had to sit the glass
    in the sun until the water warmed.

She fed the crows before her lunch and again
    after her lunch. The crows lined up
    on the wall near her locked front gate.

After she died
    I was dismissed.
    I was told to take all her stuffed crows
    to the Abiquiu dump.

2 October 2005

banco: a bench, usually made of adobe brick
chamisa: a wild shrub found in New Mexico

Evacuee

I passed him walking barefoot
        along the empty road
        far outside a desolate, wasted
        Louisiana town.

I stopped,
        turned my car around
        to offer him a ride.

I followed a dull opalescent oil-slick.

I searched a long distance,
        found no one,
        not even a shadow.

I think of him today
        as I sit in my quiet garden,
        where flowers welcome loneliness
        and pain.

12 September 2005
Galisteo, New Mexico

Waiting for the Call

If the children should call
  to ask for the set of encyclopedias
  or the family portraits,
  I would speak to them
  about learning the language
  of stones,
  about how stones learn to love
  the sculptor's chisel
  that turns marble and granite
  into a gentle lion
  or a child in a father's arms.

1 January 2006

Ripening in the Orchard
—for Dorothy Wiley

I want to be here in my orchard,
>ripening, enclosed by green apples
>and yellowing pears.

I want the comfort of being held
>in my orchard,
>held loosely,
>touched palpably
>with the expectancy
>of juicy sweetness.

In my orchard
>each apple, each pear,
>about to ripen on its branch,
>survives bees, ravaging
>squirrels, thieving magpies.

I will sit in my orchard this Fall,
>press my face into the fullness
>and pleasure of Autumn succulence,
>digest its companionship.

Join me. We will count passing clouds.

10 May 2004

Putting the Fire to Rest
—for Tom and Joan Rudholm

There will come a day
      when I cannot hear the birds,
      but I will remember them.

Their music will be the laughter
      of daughters and lovers
      played on night strings.

And when the sunrise is stolen
      I will remember the rising flame
      from the East.

There will be a week
      I will not walk my road
      among wild asters;
      their many-petalled faces
      will peer from the pores
      of my skin.

I will hold their purple faces
      next to my own and weep.

10 September 2005

Night Voices
When My Shadow Sleeps

A Poem from the Magpie
—for Jim Scoggin and Cynthia

Magpies make their poems into nests,
        gathering dreams and stolen songs together,
        filling them with chatter, exclamation marks
        and incomplete sentences.

They parade across the yard,
        beginning every word
        with a capital letter,
        leaving commas here and there.

Late at night,
        I will go out to where they paraded
        to gather up their crossword droppings
        and spend the moonlight
        jig-sawing their gifts together
        into my poem.

12 November 2005

A Gift of Stars
    —for my poet friend Cynthia West

Neruda speaks of being struck by stars,
    a voice of starlight,
    by an illumination
    more than by brightness,
    by words forming a constellation
    inviting a poem.

Stars do not rhyme.
    They stretch out
    from an unfathomable galaxy.

A poem can do that:
    stretch across distance,
    to break open Winter's coldness
    with a scent of orange
    and the pain that lies under a stone.

What arrived on this page
    is not a planned thing,
    but a plunging star,
    a sigh,
    a cry churned up by a storm,
    a cloud crashing against a mountain,
    soft breathing shared by cottonwoods
    when their leaves fall in October.

Stars have no maps, like poems.
    They fall unguided when no one is watching.

        9 October, 2005

The Archeologist as Full Moon
   —for Kurt Anschultz

Like a full moon,
        he smiled at three figures
        carved on stone, gave them names.
        Was he listening for them to give him his name?

He stared at a hunter eyeing a delicate deer
        carved on stone,
        traced their lines with an artist's eye.
        Was he imagining the hunter hunting him?

He paused, squinted at carved panels of spears,
        birds impaled on some.
        Was he noticing how the spears pointed
        up at the stars?

He knelt down to capture the bird on a stalk of corn
        carved on stone.
        Was he hearing the rustle of cornstalks
        in the valley below?
        Was he hearing the last song of that bird
        before it became stone?

He searched for carved corn, gardens or fields.
        Was he feeling his own hunger for the earth?
        Did he dream of sinking his feet into mud,
        of pressing his hand into clay
        to make a bowl for his laughter and tears?

And those shields carved on stone,
        was he feeling safe when he photographed them?
        Did he reach for his own shield
        when he saw clouds sheltering the mountain?

I watched him stepping about those carved stones.
He left nothing behind.

I wanted the flute players to bring him home,
a full moon.

19 July 2004

At Monk's Pub
—for Lisselton friends John and Kate McGrath

There is music tonight in Monk's Pub,
    nesting in my ears.

I will sit near the soft, slow peat fire.

I will see the Galway Bay red faces
    of the fishermen,

        smell the balm of manure on the shoes
        of the farmers,

        hear the Clare dialect like the clicking
        of stones when the sea comes in.

I will taste the echoes of the songs of poets.

I will drink bog-brown Guinness,
    raising my glass
    to the shadows on the wall.

7 June 2005

Ballyvaughan, County Clare, Ireland
Published 2006:
Ballydonaghue Parish Magazine,
edited by John McGrath,
Lisselton, County Kerry, Ireland

A Poet Returning Home
—*for my artist friend John Hoover and Mary*

My dreams had left raindrops on the windows,
      but the sun blinded me,
      filling my pockets with time.

I had come home with gulls' wings,
      leaving undulating stillness behind
      in the furze bush
      where no one could reach it.

My dreams had left raindrops
      running down the windows,
      broken lines of wet dots and dashes,
      a Morse code of light.

I had come home with mud on my feet
      to plant sprouting seeds
      stolen from the famine fields
      where ancestors rise up
      on moon-filled nights.

All I wanted was to write poems on the wind.

6 June 2005
Listowel, County Kerry, Ireland

The Hand on My Shoulder

What is left of the day
        as night fills this place
        is memory,
        laughter,
        a glass of wine
        and a candle.

What is left of the day
        as night calls the shapes of the moon
        and fits stars into blackness
        is the ravishing of daylight,
        the stealing of the scent of lavender,
        the giving away of songs
        birds have left behind.

What night brings
        is the unseen voices in the dust,
        the merging of dreams,
        the flutter of lost morning sighs.

What night brings
        is the blankness of unsaid words,
        the open space of walking alone,
        the hand on my shoulder
        and the kiss on my lips
        when you said goodnight
        for the last time.

11 July 2004

The Flower that Steals the Sun
—for my poet friend Janet Eigner

Looking into the center of an orange marigold,
      I see a multitude of lips,
         dry from kissing the sun.

I see crew-cut soldierly petals,
      tight medals,
         chipped fingernails of August light.

Its blue-green arm stretches
      out of the pottery pitcher,
      weaving among zinnias
      and a muscular silence
      that colors hold in sunlight.

If it were a single night bloom,
      it might blind an owl
         with its beacon of orange feathers.

There is a hole in the garden
      it came from. It leaves a ghost there
      where the sun was stolen
      where now only pale moonlight sleeps.

20 August 2005

The Fifth of July 2005

Sixteen unidentified soldiers,
lying under American flags,
woke me up.

I tossed, rolled out of bed.
The July-hot pine floor was a sun-baked desert.

I stood mute in the dark,
shackled in biting sand.

Was it the film *Farenheit 9/11*
or the fireworks at the High School
that brought those soldiers to my bed?

Burning, I fell back on the mattress,
storm-wet,
arms across my chest,
my breathing shallow.

The moon pressed against my window.

I sank into sleep.

When I awoke, the sun was rising,
dyeing my white sheets red.

6 July 2004

Where are the Words
—for poet William Witherup

I search for new, penetrating words:

    words torn from the hems of *galabiyyas*
    that have wiped blood away,

    words deciphered from sounds
    of wailing mud homes of Gaza and Dujail,

    words from humiliated men and women,
    whose light was smothered,

    words I must use in my poems
    to speak for those who cry
    before they make me deaf.

                  4—8 May 2004

galabiyya: long, loose robe worn in the Middle East

Blue of Baghdad

When the smoke clears in Baghdad,
    will people in the streets
    hold their faces up to a blue sky?

If I were there,
    I would color the world blue:
    melt my crayons,
    smear them across the stones
    where blood has dried.

I would prepare blue paint,
    pressing blue from my jeans and shirts,
    unravel and soak indigo threads
    from rugs covering empty water jars.

I would dye my *galabiyya* blue,
    as if woven from the ancient free-flowing Euphrates.

I would dress my children in blue,
    the blue of their bruises,
    blue from the fallen roof of their home.

I would paint images of blue butterflies
    on the stones around our garden.
    Perhaps the foreign soldiers
    would not target them
    when they pass by.

11 September 2005

Listening for Their Voices
—*for Ibrahim Muhamed al-Attab, Yemeni Poet*

I want to hear again and again
      voices from the Arab world.

I listen early in the morning
      before the sun calls from our minarets
      of the Sangre de Cristo Mountains.

I want to hear those voices
      while I shine apples in my orchard.

I want to hear again and again
      poems lost in the smoke of Baghdad,
      ground under the stones of Lebanon,
      unearthed in Syria and Yemen,
      lying under frayed rugs
      covering jerry-cans of water in Gaza.

I want to hear those apocalyptic voices,
      not just their echoes.

I want Fadwa Tugan of Nablis
      and Abdul Wahab al-Bayati to sing
      from Baghdad again; I want
      Sa'di Yusef to fly his poems as banners
      on the foreign tanks in Basra.

But now when Nizar Qabbani holds my hand to say:
      My grieved country.
      In a flash
      You changed me from a poet who wrote love poems
      To a poet who writes with a knife...

What we feel is beyond words:
We should be ashamed of our poems...*

I will weep with him,
gagging on his pain.

10 October 2005

* Nizar Qabbani: "Footnotes to the Book of Setbacks"
Modern Poetry of the Arab World, translated and edited
by Abdullah al-Udhari, Penguin Books Ltd., 1986

Brothers
—*for artist brothers in Abba,*
Kingdom of Saudi Arabia

When the evening news-announcer
    speaks of the death of men far away
    I call them by their names.

They burst into my kitchen,
    run through the house,
    trample my bed late at night.

I want to be with them,
    wherever they give their last breaths.

I need to help dig their graves,
    to scatter roses and jasmine,
    to steady the stones marking their graves.

I long to keep their faces in memory,
    smooth their hair,
    close their eyes.

The brothers I never had.

27 August 2004

On a Carpet of Woven Flowers
    —for Alastair Reid

I will tell you my secret.
I choose to be a prisoner of the Arabs.

I long for their carpets of woven flowers,
    to drink the splashing of their fountains.

I find my thumbprint carved in the mosque in Sana'a,
    almost rubbed smooth by poets writing love songs.

I carry the sweet scent of wet sands from the Marib oasis,
    the blowing dust of wailing in Fallujah.

Ah! To be a prisoner of the Arabs,
    waiting for my head to drop on a carpet of woven
    flowers.

                23 November 2004

To Celebrate the Dark
—for my poet friend Marie Leontine Tsibinda

I celebrate the dark
    after it has passed.
    I see clearly what has
    bumped against me,
    thumped against my chest,
    pulled wax from my ears,
    stolen words from my poems,
    replaced them with hopeful images.

After it has passed
    I recognize the gate has always been open,
    the pathway always without end,
    and the stumbling was because
    I blinded myself.

I had left my rucksack open,
    thinking I wanted the moths to fly away,
    thinking that if I let the dark
    into all the pockets,
    pulled the zipper tight,
    I would have captured it,
    made it the prisoner
    it had made of me.

After it has passed
    I celebrate the dark.
    I praise those early morning hours
    when the moon flowed West,
    erasing the stars.

In my blood
> I know the darkness will come again
> to close the door for a brief time,
> but I will have the words and colors
> to paint my home
> in sweeping strokes of fire and water.
>
> *8 August 2004*

The Longest Winter

Here was a place to sit, wait, watch,
      to think thoughts but not to voice them.

The world was crowded with moons,
      one in each mud puddle.

He had longed for a visitor,
      anyone, to open his book,
      test verbs, modify nouns.

This was the longest Winter.
      Voiceless thoughts bound his feet in fog.

He ran out of paper,
      etched incomplete sentences
      in the soft plaster of his walls.

He carved words on garden stones,
      words magpies stole when his back was turned.

Wild rabbits and foxes left notes to him
      in their tracks on clotted mud,
      which he deciphered in the morning.

At night when moon-filled puddles shimmered
      with the cold, he laid his blanket over them,
      blinding the moon.

He preferred the dark where the sounds
      of the earth breathing sang the truth
      and gave him life.

                23 March 2005

Returning to the Orchard

When I despair
>I remember an inner light
>hanging in clusters in my orchard.

I visit those trees.
>I see how apples hold the morning.

I see how they grow in secrecy,
>gathering sweetness
>when the stars are absent.

Each season, the apples draw together
>like old friends ripening.

When I despair, I return to my orchard.
>I press a single apple against my cheek.
>It burns with the song of bees.

But night arrives,
>trees are phosphorescent,
>valley dogs carry a pair of moons
>in their eyes.

19 December 2005

One Last Poem

I wrote poems to you after you left,
        when the calm was full of my courage.

        I should have said . . .
        I meant to say . . .
        I want you to know . . .
        Are you listening?

Perhaps after the first poem, you decided
        not to open any of the others that came
        week after week until my pen was dry.

I wanted you to remember the picnic
        when I made you a crown of buttercups.

        There were robins
        humming bees
        butterflies.
        Do you remember?

You sat in the sun with the crown of buttercups,
        your hair weeping
        down the side of your face.

I picked more buttercups, tossed them up in the air.

I write a poem to you now, fifty years later,
        when the buttercups, their legs cut,
        their yellow faded,
        lie scattered
        like the corpses of lightning bugs
        across our field.

23 January 2003

When My Shadow Sleeps
—for my friend Jack Di Benedetto

Hope has been hanging
      on the trees all day,
        expecting the loneliness of Autumn
      to bring strangers to my door.

I try counting sparrows
      on my fingers.
      I spend too much time
      watching birds.

There are squirrels to curse
      and valley dog to answer.
      The fence posts stare through me,
      shrivel the morning glories.

I know the well in the field
      is bottomless.

I thought I had tossed all the stones
      to the edge of the road.

When night finally comes
      to fill the chairs and tea cups,
      I will walk about alone,
      knowing my shadow has gone to sleep.

19 August 2004

I Don't Need Two Lives

It is November.
>   There are deep shadows under the apple tree.
>   The walkway stones remain free of footprints.

Words run circles around trees.
>   They form sentences in the mud
>   that describe what is lost.

If I count the leaves caught in rose bushes,
>   I'll know the distance from Winter
>   to where you live.

The fingerprints on my paper
>   spiral into letters and photographs.
>   I'll walk with deer into the orchard at sunset.

I don't need two lives.
>   I'll continue to write my poems.
>   I want to die writing.

27 November 2004

Learning About Fire

What will consume me before death?

If I place my hands in yours,
    our blood will mingle
    with the fire in mica,
    the hard redness of granite.

If I wade into pools of light
    that lie under ripening September
    to become pear bark
    and magpie nest twigs,
    I will have prepared myself for burning.

If I howl at the moon in deserts
    of white sands, I will have uttered
    scorched words my eyes could never say
    to crowds.

If I put my pen down without writing
    a word of praise
    to the scent of mint,
    to the taste of salt on your morning neck,
    I will never know fire.

20 August 2005

In the Sounds of Light
—for my poet friend Jane Lipman

Listen!

This morning's ecstatic sun is flowing
      into your windows,
        giving holiness to your rooms.

At noon you will hear the stillness of birds
      waiting for the sun to begin its descent
      in the West, where the mountain lies,
      eager for its caress.

At night when children say their prayers,
      the vanishing sun hears the colors of flowers,
      feels the waving of trees
      at its departure.

Listen!

The wanton moon comes over the mountain,
      so indecisive, waxing and waning.

It treads lightly after the sun.

Look for its tracks in the dust today
      where you left your footsteps.

We don't want the sun and the moon to die.

              12 October 2005

He Died Before I Could Hold Him

How many times did we say good-bye?

He enters my heart where all the silence
     is filled with his lonely wildness.

I hear his rippled laughter
     when he ran cold, shivering from the river.

He interrupts every song
     that summer colors leave behind
     in the morning garden.

There is no room for us
     in the bells of tulips.

He was all the music I needed to breathe.

I hear him snapping his brightness
     in the blazing fireplace.
         He leaves whispers in the ashes.

He colors every room
     in the memory-blue
     of holding hands
     between the pages of poetry.

If I sit long enough,
     the sounds that scuff across the floor
     vanish into fog that being too young
     sighs along the ground.

Now he arrives when the moon rises.
     He carries it in his arms
     when he knocks on my door.

How many times did we say good-bye?

There are questions that migrating birds
    ask when they are lost.

There are voices like mine
    that sit in trees
        just before the saw cuts them down.

7 February 2006

In Remembrance

When it is over,
      the applause,
      the firm handshake,
      the presentation of flowers,
      the day will hold questions:
      when did it begin,
      why did it take so long,
      why were there such tantalizing gift-wrappings?

11 July 2002

The Last Word of My Pen
—in memory of my beloved friend Nita Finney

If I touch the edge of your ear
    with the last word of my pen,
    do not pull away.

I want to steal a taste of honey
    from the hive of abundance
    you have stored since childhood.

I will spread delight across the face
    of the world,
    cutting through the clouds.

2 July 2005
Galisteo, New Mexico

ABOUT THE POET

James McGrath, poet, visual artist and teacher, is known for his narrative poetry in the KAET/PBS American Indian Artist Series in the 1970s. He has published poetry in 15 anthologies, including *Dakotah Territory, Passager, Inside Grief, In Cabin Six, Mercy of Tides,* and *Sacred Waters,* and a collection of poems, *At the Edgelessness of Light,* also from Sunstone Press, among others. McGrath was poet-artist-in-residence with the United States Information Service, Arts America in Yemen, Kingdom of Saudi Arabia and the Republic of the Congo in the 1990s and his 50 year retrospective as artist was held at the Meridian Gallery in San Francisco in 2002. He lives in La Cieneguilla, Santa Fe, New Mexico.

This book of poetry has been printed on acid free paper.
The typeface is Warnock Pro Display and
Warnock Pro Bold Caption.

www.ingramcontent.com/pod-product-compliance
Lightning Source LLC
Chambersburg PA
CBHW021012090426
738CB00007B/767

Learning About Fire

What will consume me before death?

If I place my hands in yours,
      our blood will mingle
      with the fire in mica,
      the hard redness of granite.

If I wade into pools of light
      that lie under ripening September
      to become pear bark
      and magpie nest twigs,
      I will have prepared myself for burning.

If I howl at the moon in deserts
      of white sands, I will have uttered
      scorched words my eyes could never say
      to crowds.

If I put my pen down without writing
      a word of praise
      to the scent of mint,
      to the taste of salt on your morning neck,
      I will never know fire.

20 August 2005

In the Sounds of Light
    —for my poet friend Jane Lipman

Listen!

This morning's ecstatic sun is flowing
        into your windows,
        giving holiness to your rooms.

At noon you will hear the stillness of birds
        waiting for the sun to begin its descent
        in the West, where the mountain lies,
        eager for its caress.

At night when children say their prayers,
        the vanishing sun hears the colors of flowers,
        feels the waving of trees
        at its departure.

Listen!

The wanton moon comes over the mountain,
        so indecisive, waxing and waning.

It treads lightly after the sun.

Look for its tracks in the dust today
        where you left your footsteps.

We don't want the sun and the moon to die.

                12 October 2005

He Died Before I Could Hold Him

How many times did we say good-bye?

He enters my heart where all the silence
      is filled with his lonely wildness.

I hear his rippled laughter
      when he ran cold, shivering from the river.

He interrupts every song
      that summer colors leave behind
      in the morning garden.

There is no room for us
      in the bells of tulips.

He was all the music I needed to breathe.

I hear him snapping his brightness
      in the blazing fireplace.
        He leaves whispers in the ashes.

He colors every room
      in the memory-blue
      of holding hands
      between the pages of poetry.

If I sit long enough,
      the sounds that scuff across the floor
      vanish into fog that being too young
      sighs along the ground.

Now he arrives when the moon rises.
      He carries it in his arms
      when he knocks on my door.

How many times did we say good-bye?

There are questions that migrating birds
    ask when they are lost.

There are voices like mine
    that sit in trees
        just before the saw cuts them down.

7 February 2006

In Remembrance

When it is over,
    the applause,
    the firm handshake,
    the presentation of flowers,
    the day will hold questions:
    when did it begin,
    why did it take so long,
    why were there such tantalizing gift-wrappings?

11 July 2002

The Last Word of My Pen
—in memory of my beloved friend Nita Finney

If I touch the edge of your ear
    with the last word of my pen,
    do not pull away.

I want to steal a taste of honey
    from the hive of abundance
    you have stored since childhood.

I will spread delight across the face
    of the world,
    cutting through the clouds.

2 July 2005
Galisteo, New Mexico

ABOUT THE POET

James McGrath, poet, visual artist and teacher, is known for his narrative poetry in the KAET/PBS American Indian Artist Series in the 1970s. He has published poetry in 15 anthologies, including *Dakotah Territory, Passager, Inside Grief, In Cabin Six, Mercy of Tides,* and *Sacred Waters*, and a collection of poems, *At the Edgelessness of Light,* also from Sunstone Press, among others. McGrath was poet-artist-in-residence with the United States Information Service, Arts America in Yemen, Kingdom of Saudi Arabia and the Republic of the Congo in the 1990s and his 50 year retrospective as artist was held at the Meridian Gallery in San Francisco in 2002. He lives in La Cieneguilla, Santa Fe, New Mexico.

This book of poetry has been printed on acid free paper.
The typeface is Warnock Pro Display and
Warnock Pro Bold Caption.

www.ingramcontent.com/pod-product-compliance
Lightning Source LLC
Chambersburg PA
CBHW021012090426
42738CB00007B/767